MW00715043

BLESSED BE
YOUR
NAME
DEVOTIONAL

Devotions Inspired by the Song

HONOR HB BOOKS

Inspiration and Motivation for the Season of Life

COOK COMMUNICATIONS MINISTRIES
Colorado Springs, Colorado • Paris, Ontario
KINGSWAY COMMUNICATIONS LTD
Eastbourne, England

Honor® is an imprint of
Cook Communications Ministries, Colorado Springs, CO 80918
Cook Communications, Paris, Ontario
Kingsway Communications, Eastbourne, England

BLESSED BE YOUR NAME

Cover Design: BMB Design/Scott Johnson

First Printing, 2005
Printed in Canada

2 3 4 5 6 7 8 9 10 Printing/Year 10 09 08 07 06 05

Library of Congress Cataloging-in-Publication Data

Palmer, Adam, 1975-
  Blessed be Your name : devotions inspired by the song / [Adam Palmer].
     p. cm. -- (30 days of worship)
  ISBN 1-56292-717-5
 1. Hymns--Devotional use. 2. Devotional calendars. I. Title. II. Series.
  BV340
  264'.23--dc22

                              2005020788

Introduction

We hear God's name in a variety of ways these days. Off-the-cuff exclamations, epithets, prayers, sermons … God's name is seemingly everywhere.

But do we treasure it? Do we feel about God's name the same way he does?

God's name is a multi-layered, multi-faceted word. It is full of power, dignity, reverence, grace, honor, and might. It is an adjective, describing his character. It is a verb, acting on our behalf. It is a noun, upon which we may call in our most desperate times.

Written by Matt and Beth Redman, the song "Blessed Be Your Name" touches on God's name and the many meanings it contains. This devotional, based on the much-loved song, was created to help you learn more about God's name and all it entails. As you read over the next thirty days, endeavor to learn all you can about the name of God.

As you go through the pages of this book, may you learn to revere God's name in the same way he does. May "Blessed Be Your Name" become more than just lyrics and melody to you; may it be a reminder of the depth, height, length, and breadth of the wonderful name of God.

Blessed Be Your Name

By **Matt and Beth Redman**

Blessed be your name
In the land that is plentiful
Where your streams of abundance flow
Blessed be your name

Blessed be your name
When I'm found in the desert place
Though I walk through the wilderness
Blessed be your name

Every blessing you pour out, I turn back to
praise
When the darkness closes in, Lord,
Still I will say
Blessed be the name of the Lord
Blessed be your name

Blesses be the name of the Lord
Blessed be your glorious name

Blessed be your name
When the sun's shining down on me
When the world's all as it should be
Blessed be your name

Blessed be your name
On the road marked with suffering
Though there's pain in the offering
Blessed be your name

You give and take away
You give and take away
My heart will choose to say
Lord, blessed be your name

DAY 1: Blessed Be Your Name

*Moses said to God, "Suppose I go to the Israelites and say to
them, 'The God of your fathers has sent me to you,' and
they ask me, 'What is his name?' Then what shall I tell
them?" God said to Moses, "I AM WHO I AM. This is what you
are to say to the Israelites: 'I AM has sent me to you.'" God
also said to Moses, "Say to the Israelites, 'The LORD, the God
of your fathers—the God of Abraham, the God of Isaac and*

the God of Jacob—has sent me to you.' This is my name forever, the name by which I am to be remembered from generation to generation."

—Exodus 3:13–15

God's name is historic.

Shakespeare's Romeo uttered the famous line, "What's in a name? A rose by any other name would smell as sweet." Romeo, of course, was full of star-crossed optimism about love and didn't really know what he was talking about.

In God's view of things, a name is very important. In response to Romeo's rhetorical question, "What's in a name?" God would answer, "Everything."

From the time he spoke light into existence until now—and beyond—God has been making a name for himself. A name that is synonymous with blessings. Synonymous with triumph. Synonymous with redemption. God's name is an encapsulation of all he has done throughout the ages and all that he will do as time progresses. His name is his entire essence, the one thing by which he is to be remembered from generation to generation.

When we remember the history of God's name and the things he's done for people like Abraham and Isaac and Jacob, we bless that very name. He was faithful to those men and to countless other people in the Bible. He will repeat history and be faithful to us.

His name is our everything.

Prayer for the Day:

Dear Lord, help me to remember what your name means. As I embark on this study of your name, I pray that you will help me to have a greater love for it than I've ever had before. Teach me to treasure your name, and help me to remember all that your name stands for, so that it will be a light to me in the midst of my darkness. I bless your name, Lord.

AMEN.

DAY 2: In the Land That Is Plentiful

On the evening of the fourteenth day of the month, while camped at Gilgal on the plains of Jericho, the Israelites celebrated the Passover. The day after the Passover, that very day, they ate some of the produce of the land: unleavened bread and roasted grain. The manna stopped the day after they ate this food from the land; there was no longer any manna for the Israelites, but that year they ate of the produce of Canaan.

—JOSHUA 5:10–12

God's name can be relied upon.

The Israelites had just spent the last forty years of their existence wandering through the desert. Before that, they'd been enslaved in Egypt. God had sent Moses to deliver them and bring them to the Promised Land of Canaan, which they were now on the brink of entering.

As a means of sustaining them in the wilderness, God provided manna, thin wafers of food that appeared daily. Having no other options, the Israelites relied on God for their sustenance.

But now they were in Canaan, and God no longer needed to provide manna. The Israelites no longer needed to rely on him for food—it was already there, as part of the land. No, now they needed to rely on God for something entirely different.

Canaan was already occupied.

Now the task for the Israelites changed from just surviving to overcoming. They had to overcome their enemies in order to possess the land, and they would need every bit of strength and confidence they could get from God.

In other words, their wilderness days were behind them, but their reliance days were still with them. The plentiful land meant they had to call on God's name for an entirely different reason than they had before.

Fortunately, God's name is one we can all rely upon, no matter what circumstance we're facing.

Prayer for the Day:

Dear God, teach me to rely on your name. I pray that you'll give me the strength and confidence I need to walk through this day. Prompt me to call on your name no matter what circumstances I face. I know I can count on you, God. You've never failed me before, and you never will. You are the Ultimate Reliance.

AMEN.

DAY 3:
Where Your Streams of Abundance Flow

The whole Israelite community set out from the Desert of Sin, traveling from place to place as the LORD commanded. They camped at Rephidim, but there was no water for the people to drink. So they quarreled with Moses and said, "Give us water to drink." Moses replied, "Why do you quarrel with me? Why do you put the LORD to the test?" But the people were thirsty for water there, and they grumbled against Moses. They said, "Why did you bring us up out of Egypt to make us and our children and livestock die of thirst?" Then Moses cried out to the LORD, "What am I to do with these people? They are almost ready to stone me." The LORD answered Moses, "Walk on ahead of the people. Take with you some of the elders of Israel and take in your hand the staff with which you struck the Nile, and go. I will stand there before you by the rock at Horeb. Strike the rock, and water will come out of it for the people to drink." So Moses did this in the sight of the elders of Israel. And he called the place Massah and Meribah because the Israelites quarreled and because they tested the LORD saying, "Is the LORD among us or not?"

—**Exodus 17:1–7**

God's name is not dependent on our trust.

It's easy to wonder sometimes why God ever put up with the Israelites. This passage records events that took place while they were still wandering in the desert. Even though they'd seen God's miraculous hand bring deliverance from their Egyptian slavery, they still doubted his methods and his purpose.

So there they were with a great need, and instead of calling on God's name they start getting angry with Moses, as if he was their provider and not God. We can even see how fed up Moses is—imagine him throwing his hands up in frustration as he says to God,

"What am I supposed to do with these people? Come on. This is ridiculous!"

Nevertheless, thanks to Moses' prayers on their behalf, God had mercy on his chosen people even though they were completely in the wrong. God provided a stream of abundance, not because the Israelites or Moses talked him into it, but because that's just his character.

It's part of his name.

We don't earn God's provision because we're so nice to him. We partake of it because he loves us—even when we don't merit it.

His streams of abundance flow because that's who he is. Faithful, even when we aren't.

Prayer for the Day:

O Lord, I thank you for your streams of abundance flowing through all my desert places. I thank you, God, that you see me in the midst of my wilderness and that you provide for me even when I don't necessarily deserve it. Help me to speak your name first, not the name of anyone or anything else. Blessed be your name, Lord. Blessed be your name.

AMEN.

DAY 4: Blessed Be Your Name

Then the LORD said to Moses, "Get up early in the morning, confront Pharaoh and say to him, 'This is what the LORD, the God of the Hebrews, says: Let my people go, so that they may worship me, or this time I will send the full force of my plagues against you and against your officials and your people, so you may know that there is no one like me in all the earth. For by now I could have stretched out my hand and struck you and your people with a plague that would have wiped you off the earth. But I have raised you up for this very purpose, that I might show you my power and that my name might be proclaimed in all the earth. You still set yourself against my people and will not let them go.'"

—EXODUS 9:13–17

God's name is just.

The past couple of days have focused on the Israelites' time in the wilderness. As we journey even further back in history, we examine the end of the Israelites' time of slavery to the Egyptians.

In this passage, God has already sent a few plagues to torment Pharaoh and the Egyptians, with the express purpose of showing his power and proclaiming his name throughout the earth. Pharaoh has been resistant to God's demand of releasing the Israelites, and so now God sends Moses with yet another warning.

But this time God promises through Moses that the forthcoming plagues will be far worse than any of the ones the Egyptians have already experienced. God had been holding back for the first six plagues, but for the remaining four plagues he was going to send the full force of his power against Egypt.

Why? Because he's just. The Israelites were his chosen people, and they'd been mistreated by the Egyptians for the past four hundred years. God, in his justice, knew that the time had come for his people to be released. But

Pharaoh, fearing his own safety, was foolishly ignoring the warnings.

We know from our past few days of study that the Israelites eventually received their freedom, but not before God's justice had been served on Pharaoh and God's name had been proclaimed in all the earth as one worthy of worship.

This powerful God, who has the ability to send the full force of plagues against an entire nation, has given us the honor of calling upon his just name. He will ensure justice on our behalf.

Prayer for the Day:

Heavenly Father, I thank you for your just name. I thank you that you see me when I am mistreated and that no injustice escapes your watchful eye. I pray that your name would be proclaimed in my world, and that all would see your justice in my life—as you see fit, Lord.

AMEN.

DAY 5: Blessed Be Your Name

You shall not misuse the name of the LORD your God, for the LORD will not hold anyone guiltless who misuses his name.

—EXODUS 20:7

God's name is precious.

When God gave the people of Israel their first law, he began with the Ten Commandments. And one of those commandments was this one: Don't misuse God's name. It's right up there with the commandments not to murder and not to commit adultery.

Misuse is a big deal.

Why? Because God's name is precious. As we discussed earlier, it is the complete summation of who he is. It is powerful—the name that is above all other names. It is not something to be bandied about. Instead it is something to be treasured.

Most of us have a treasured heirloom some-where in our house—something that holds many special memories for us, that reminds us of simpler times. And because of everything that heirloom means, most of us keep it in a place of honor. It won't soon become an impromptu doorstop or paperweight. It won't be involved in a game of catch in the backyard. It won't be thrown in a fit of anger. No, that heirloom is treated with utmost care because it is precious.

In the same way, we are to treasure God's name and never misuse it.

His name is far too precious to be used flippantly or in anger. Let us treasure it. For it is to be treasured.

Prayer for the Day:

Sweet Lord God, I thank you for your precious, precious name. First and foremost, I repent of taking your name too lightly and for misusing it. Forgive me, Lord, for disobeying your commands. I pray that you'll give me discernment so that I may always use your name properly. Help me to treasure your name, Lord, and never to slander it or drag it through the mud by my actions. Thank you.

AMEN.

DAY 6:
When I'm Found in the Desert Place

The LORD's anger was aroused that day and he swore this oath: "Because they have not followed me wholeheartedly, not one of the men twenty years old or more who came up out of Egypt will see the land I promised on oath to Abraham, Isaac and Jacob—not one except Caleb son of Jephunneh the Kenizzite and Joshua son of Nun, for they followed the LORD wholeheartedly." The LORD's anger burned against Israel and he made them wander in the desert forty years, until the whole generation of those who had done evil in his sight was gone.

—NUMBERS 32:10–13

God's name is gracious.

Let's go back to the Israelites wandering in the desert. They'd made their way across the wilderness and were on the edge of the land God had promised to them, the land of Canaan. Moses sent spies into the land, one from each of the twelve tribes of Israel, and the spies came back with the report that the land was occupied by giants.

Ten of the men said there was no way the Israelites would be able to take the land, but Caleb and Joshua said it was a good land, and if God wanted to give it to them, then they would be able to take it.

Guess who the Israelites believed?

Despite all the overwhelming evidence to the contrary, the people panicked and decided then and there that God had sent them to their deaths by sending them to Canaan. They were certain that they were going to lose the fight. So God told them in no uncertain terms that because of their unbelief they would not be allowed to enter into Canaan. Instead, they were going to wander the desert for a while until the unbelieving generation died.

God didn't suddenly revoke the land from them, though he certainly could have. Instead, he had grace upon the descendants of those in the wilderness and allowed them to go in and possess the land.

What can we learn from this? Even when we sin and do wrong, even when we doubt God's name, he is still good and his name is still holy. He was true to his word in this story, and he'll be true to his word in our individual stories.

And when we forget that, he lovingly offers his gracious name and allows us the opportunity to repent and possess the land we were meant to live in.

Prayer for the Day:

God, I thank you for your grace. Please forgive me for the times I've doubted that your grace was sufficient for my troubles. I thank you that your grace abounds toward me, and I pray that you'll help me to live like Joshua and Caleb, not like the ten other spies. I want to follow you wholeheartedly, God.

AMEN.

DAY 7:
Though
I Walk
through the
Wilderness

Then Jesus was led by the Spirit into the desert to be tempted by the devil. After fasting forty days and forty nights, he was hungry. The tempter came to him and said, "If you are the Son of God, tell these stones to become bread." Jesus answered, "It is written: 'Man does not live on bread alone, but on every word that comes from the mouth of God.'" Then the devil took him to the holy city and had him stand on the highest point of the temple. "If you are the Son of God," he said, "throw yourself down.

For it is written: 'He will command his angels concerning you, and they will lift you up in their hands, so that you will not strike your foot against a stone.'" Jesus answered him, "It is also written: 'Do not put the Lord your God to the test.'"Again, the devil took him to a very high mountain and showed him all the kingdoms of the world and their splendor. "All this I will give you," he said, "if you will bow down and worship me." Jesus said to him, "Away from me, Satan! For it is written: 'Worship the Lord your God, and serve him only.'" Then the devil left him, and angels came and attended him.

—**Matthew 4:1–11**

God's name is potent in the midst of temptation.

Forty days and nights. That's a long time to go with no food. Most of us get pretty weak if we skip breakfast or miss lunch, but Jesus was going toe to toe with the Devil with his stomach most likely emptier than we've ever experienced.

Then the Devil came bringing all manners of temptations to Jesus in an attempt to swerve him from his course of redemption. But Jesus had an answer for everything the Devil tried to use against him, and those answers came directly from previously recorded Scripture.

In a sense, Jesus was using God's name against the Devil. The Scriptures Jesus used are the history of God and how mankind is to react to him. "Live on the words of God." "Don't test God." "Worship only God." Each quote uses God's name with powerful effect.

God's name, as reflected in his Word, is a potent ally in the midst of tempting circumstances. It is a name the Devil fears, especially when we call upon it as he is attempting to trip us up.

Jesus used God's name when he was tempted; it only makes sense for us to do the same. Blessed be that mighty, mighty name.

Prayer for the Day:

Lord God, I thank you for your name; that you've provided a way out of temptation by giving me the ability to call on your name. Help me to follow your example, Jesus, when I find myself in the midst of temptation. Teach me to call on your name. Help me to remember the words you've spoken. Help me, Jesus.

AMEN.

DAY 8: Blessed Be Your Name

David said to the Philistine, "You come against me with sword and spear and javelin, but I come against you in the name of the LORD Almighty, the God of the armies of Israel, whom you have defied. This day the LORD will hand you over to me, and I'll strike you down and cut off your head. Today I will give the carcasses of the Philistine army to the birds of the air and the beasts of the earth, and the whole world will know that there is a God in Israel. All those gathered here will know that it is not by sword or spear that the LORD saves; for the battle is the LORD's, and he will give all of you into our hands."

—1 SAMUEL 17:45–47

God's name is mighty in battle.

We all know the story of David and Goliath. David was small and young; Goliath was gigantic and experienced. But David took down the giant from long range with one stone from his sling, defeating Goliath and all his mighty armor and weaponry.

The key to David's victory is found in this passage. As a shepherd boy, David had many opportunities to practice using his sling to ward off predators. Earlier in this chapter, he tells King Saul how God had protected him as he guarded his flock against a lion and a bear.

David had courage because he knew God was on his side. Because he knew God fought his battles for him.

So with this knowledge, notice the first words David says to Goliath. "I come against you in the name of the LORD Almighty, the God of the armies of Israel, whom you have defied." David isn't fighting Goliath for any old reason—he's fighting because Goliath had insulted the name of God.

And because of that, David knew Goliath didn't stand a chance. This battle was bigger than David—it was God's. God would show Goliath—and all the other Philistines—exactly how mighty his name was.

God's name is mighty in our battles too. We must simply give those battles to the Lord, so that he may prove his might.

Prayer for the Day:

God, thank you for your mighty, mighty name. I bless that name. I pray that you will give me the courage and strength to call on your name when I face spiritual Goliaths that insult and defy you. Remind me of this story, Lord, and how you fought for David. I know you'll also fight for me, for you are mighty. Blessed be your name.

AMEN.

DAY 9:
Every Blessing You Pour Out I'll Turn Back to Praise

Give thanks to the LORD, call on his name; make known among the nations what he has done. Sing to him, sing praise to him; tell of all his wonderful acts. Glory in his holy name; let the hearts of those who seek the LORD rejoice. Look to the LORD and his strength; seek his face always. Remember the wonders he has done, his miracles, and the judgments he pronounced, O descendants of Israel his servant, O sons of Jacob, his chosen ones.

—1 CHRONICLES 16:8–13

God's name is wonderful.

Sometimes we're called to praise God for no other reason than the fact that he's so wonderful. Today's passage is a praise song written by King David. In it we are exhorted to sing to God, to call on his name, and get the message out about how great God is.

But how good at this are we, really? How often do we forget God's wonders? How often do we get wrapped up in the pace of life and forget to praise him? Instead we plunge ourselves into whatever reality show we're currently watching or whatever sporting event is coming on this afternoon or how much the grass needs mowing or what we're going to eat for dinner or any of a thousand other things.

It's easy to get sidetracked. It's easy to be blinded to his wonder and forget how miraculous and just he really is.

He is wonderful.

God is worth singing about to all the nations. He has widespread, worldwide fame. And yet he answers us when we call on his name. How amazing. How awesome.

He's blessed us infinitely. We don't deserve him, but he deserves our praise.

Prayer for the Day:

Lord, I thank you for being so wonderful to me. I thank you for all your awesome acts and for your holy name. I take this moment to pause and remember the things you've done for me. Help me to keep these things fresh in my mind so that I might be able to maintain your perspective. I rejoice in your wonderful name and turn your blessings back into praise.

AMEN.

DAY 10:
Every Blessing You Pour Out I'll Turn Back to Praise

Speak to one another with psalms, hymns and spiritual songs. Sing and make music in your heart to the Lord, always giving thanks to God the Father for everything, in the name of our Lord Jesus Christ.

—EPHESIANS 5:19–20

God's name is for everyone.

When we think of "blessings," we tend to think of our homes, our families, our friends. Maybe we think of our health, the pleasant weather we're experiencing, or our jobs.

But how often do we think of other Christians?

In this passage, Paul encourages us as Christians to interact with one another as part of our worship. We are each other's blessings, and for every blessing that we receive from each other, we need to turn that blessing back into praise.

We are able to lift each other up, speak to each other about godly matters, hold each other accountable, support each other in whatever way is necessary. God has blessed us richly with a great cloud of other people who are striving for the same thing.

God calls us to worship together, to use our worship as a way of reaching into each other's lives. We must stand together in thankfulness to God for everything he has given us, corporately and individually.

And we're told to do it in the name of the Lord Jesus Christ. Blessed be that name.

Prayer for the Day:

Dear Jesus, I thank you so much for my fellow Christians who are striving beside me. I thank you for blessing me with them and for allowing me to be a blessing to them. Help me to lean on these blessings you've surrounded me with, so that together we might bless your name. I praise you, Jesus.

AMEN.

DAY 11:
When the Darkness Closes in, Lord

Who among you fears the LORD and obeys the word of his servant? Let him who walks in the dark, who has no light, trust in the name of the LORD and rely on his God.

—ISAIAH 50:10

God's name is light.

What child hasn't been afraid of the dark at least once in his life? We've all hidden under the covers at bedtime, afraid of monsters under the bed and wishing for just a little bit of light to ease our fears.

Even as adults, complete darkness can be unsettling. There's something comforting about even the slightest illumination when we must be in dark places. It eases the fear of the unknown that the dark brings with it, that vague notion that something unpleasant can happen to us at any time.

Fortunately, God is there for us when the darkness closes in on us.

We know that we can trust in his name, for his name illuminates our darkness.

Darkness comes in many forms. The darkness of sin. The darkness of fear. The darkness of lack. When the Enemy's darkness begins to squeeze us, when it threatens to wrap itself around our throats and suffocate us, we can call on God's name to invade the darkness.

The darkness closes in, but God's light overcomes and displaces the darkness.

Prayer for the Day:

Lord God, I bless your light-filled name. Thank you so much for caring enough to step into my personal darkness and shine your light on my life. I pray that you'll help me to journey in your light. Light my path, Lord; keep me where I need to be. I thank you and praise you, Lord.

AMEN.

DAY 12: Still I Will Say

Not to us, O Lord, not to us but to your name be the glory, because of your love and faithfulness.

—Psalm 115:1

God's name is singular.

The mind is a tricky place. Often, our minds can go haywire with all sorts of information, our thoughts bouncing sporadically from topic to topic. The mind can become a vast blender of different viewpoints and opinions as we wrestle with deciding how we really feel, think, or believe about something in particular.

But there's something about talking that crystallizes what's going on in our heads. Just hearing your own voice making a point tends to give that point validity and move other points slightly to the background. Hopefully, this puts us on a path of being able to say what we really mean.

Like saying that we really believe that God is God and we are nothing by comparison. Only he deserves the glory. Only his name is the one we should give glory to, not our own names or the names of anything else on this planet.

Wanting exaltation is just part of being human. Everyone wants to receive glory over something she has accomplished in life. But we cannot receive glory that is due to God—that is usurping glory that we don't deserve.

So we say the glory goes to him. By saying it, we make it more concrete in our hearts. And we remind ourselves who really deserves it.

Blessed be his name, and to him—and only him—be the glory.

Prayer for the Day:

Lord God, blessed be your name. I'm sorry, and I repent right now for any time that I've tried to take glory away from you and given it to myself, Lord. I pray that you'll help me always to point the glory directly at you. Teach me to use my words to glorify you and not me. May I live for you. I say that your name is blessed. You deserve all the glory and honor and praise.

AMEN.

DAY 13:
Blessed
Be the
Name of
the Lord

The LORD said to Moses, "Tell Aaron and his sons to treat with respect the sacred offerings the Israelites consecrate to me, so they will not profane my holy name. I am the LORD."

—LEVITICUS 22:1–2

God's name is sacred.

We hear God's name misused all over the place these days. From entertainment to casual conversation, the name of the Lord is being thrown around as an exclamation, a swear word, a punch line ... you name it.

But in the Old Testament, when the nation of Israel was being established, God had something different in mind. His name is to be respected. It is not to be profaned. It is to be held sacred.

Aaron and his sons were the first priests to minister to the Lord, so this commandment from God was something they paid attention to, as did all subsequent priests throughout Israel's history. God was serious about the sanctity of his name, which means the priests were serious about it.

Back then, priests were the only ones allowed beyond the veil that separated the presence of God from the rest of the world. But Jesus gave us access to that very place when he died on the cross. We have the same privileges as the priests.

We should show the same respect for God's name that the priests did. We must hold it sacred, for it is holy. It is respected. It is blessed.

Prayer for the Day:

God, thank you for the privilege of even speaking your name. Teach me to have the same reverence for your name that the early priests did. I repent of all the times I've profaned your name by throwing it around. I praise you, Lord, and I worship you. I bless your sacred name, God.

AMEN.

DAY 14: Blessed Be Your Name

"This, then, is how you should pray: 'Our Father in heaven, hallowed be your name, your kingdom come, your will be done on earth as it is in heaven. Give us today our daily bread. Forgive us our debts, as we also have forgiven our debtors. And lead us not into temptation, but deliver us from the evil one.'"

—Matthew 6:9–13

God's name is the beginning of all worship.

Jesus knew a thing or two about prayer. In this passage, Jesus was in the midst of an extended sermon that touched on numerous topics including the topic of prayer. Jesus offered up this model of prayer that we know as the Lord's Prayer.

Examining the structure of Jesus' model, we find that before seeking deliverance from temptation, before seeking forgiveness, before seeking physical provision—before any of these important things—we are to bless the name of God.

For God's name is the beginning of everything. It all begins with his name. By starting with God's name, we are acknowledging all that he is. We are calling on every attribute God possesses. His name encompasses all that has gone before us, so it only makes sense to start every prayer, every act of worship by blessing God's name.

And if that isn't reason enough for us to begin with his name, perhaps we should do it because Jesus modeled this specific prayer for us.

Jesus' prayer began by blessing the name of God. Our prayers and worship should start there too.

Prayer for the Day:

Lord God, I bless your name. It is holy. It is everything. Before I ask you for anything, Lord, I simply bless your holy name. Please teach me to maintain proper priorities in my prayer life, and help me to remember all that your name encompasses. Remind me to look to your name first.

AMEN.

DAY 15:
Blessed
Be the
Name of
the Lord

Do not turn away after useless idols. They can do you no good, nor can they rescue you, because they are useless. For the sake of his great name the LORD will not reject his people, because the LORD was pleased to make you his own.

—1 SAMUEL 12:21–22

God's name is direction.

We've all gone on long-distance drives before. Let's imagine for a moment that we're in the middle of the United States and we desperately need to get to the east coast. What direction would we drive?

It isn't a trick question—we would drive roughly east, along the best path to reach our destination. We wouldn't head due west because we'd eventually wind up on the wrong coastline, farther away from our original destination than we were when we started.

We wouldn't be doing ourselves much good if we headed due north or due south. We would eventually wind up in foreign countries, which would definitely prevent us from reaching our destination.

No, those directions would be useless, much like the idols God warns us to stay away from. In the same way that driving in the wrong direction is a mistake, turning away from the name of the Lord is also a mistake.

When we turn away from God and his direction-giving name, we are turning only to useless entertainments that will do us no good. Instead, we must keep ourselves focused on his wonderful name.

His name is both the destination and the map. His name is constant, and though our fickle attentions may occasionally turn from him, he will never turn away from us.

May his name guide us on.

Prayer for the Day:

Lord God, blessed be your name. Sometimes I get distracted, God, by the things of this world. I pray that you'll help me to rely on you for your direction. Teach me to keep my focus solely on you and not on the useless things that lie around me. Give me direction this day, Lord, so that I might end it a little closer to you.

AMEN.

DAY 16:
Blessed
Be Your
Glorious
Name

Then Moses said to him, "If your Presence does not go with us, do not send us up from here. How will anyone know that you are pleased with me and with your people unless you go with us? What else will distinguish me and your people from all the other people on the face of the earth?" And the LORD said to Moses, "I will do the very thing you have asked, because I am pleased with you and I know you by name." Then Moses said, "Now show me your glory." And the LORD said, "I will cause all my goodness to pass in front of you, and I will proclaim my name, the LORD, in your presence. I will have mercy on whom I will have mercy, and I will have compassion on whom I will have compassion."

—Exodus 33:15–19

God's name is glorious.

Imagine being in Moses' position here. To hear God say that he was pleased with you and that he knows you by name. Amazing. And then to have your request to see God's glory honored … even more amazing. Astounding. Astonishing.

So Moses saw God in his full glory. And what did that entail?

Hearing God's name. Out loud. From God.

How glorious must God's name be, for Moses to request it? A big part of experiencing God's glory was simply hearing his name, something which we easily take for granted in this world.

But for Moses, it was, perhaps, the highlight of his time on earth. God's name. Proclaimed before him. It was his request, and we can be assured that Moses didn't feel let down by the experience.

O, that we would treasure God's name in the same way!

God's name is glorious, the pinnacle of everything, the key to his essence. May we feel rewarded each time we hear it. It is blessed, indeed.

Prayer for the Day:

God, blessed be your glorious name. I'm sorry, Lord, if I have failed to realize how glorious your name really is on this earth. Teach me to treasure your name, Lord. Help me to defend the glory of your name when it has been mis-used. Give me the boldness and determination I need to uphold your name as the most glori-ous name ever spoken.

AMEN.

DAY 17: Blessed Be Your Name

"My father David had it in his heart to build a temple for the Name of the LORD, the God of Israel. But the LORD said to my father David, 'Because it was in your heart to build a temple for my Name, you did well to have this in your heart. Nevertheless, you are not the one to build the temple, but your son, who is your own flesh and blood—he is the one who will build the temple for my Name.' "The LORD has kept the promise he made: I have succeeded David my father and now I sit on the throne of Israel, just as the LORD promised, and I have built the temple for the Name of the LORD, the God of Israel."

—1 KINGS 8:17–20

God's name is trustworthy.

Known as Israel's greatest king, David had a dream in his heart—to build a permanent home for God to reside in. He wanted to build a magnificent temple for God, a place that would far outdo the tentlike structure that was currently in use. But David wasn't meant to do that; his son was.

So God promised David that Solomon would fulfill his dream of building the temple. And that promise was kept. Solomon did indeed head up the construction of a temple for the name of the Lord, and David's wish was carried out.

When God makes a promise, he keeps it.

Unfortunately, the same cannot be said of us. However, even though we fail in our promises, God never fails in his. He means what he says, and he will always, always, always be true to his word. He will always be true to his name.

Because his name is trustworthy.

When we encounter things in life we'd like to see—temples we'd like to build—we know we can always rely on God to fulfill the promises he's made to us. We know we can trust him with anything.

It's all in his name.

Prayer for the Day:

God, I pray that you will help me trust you completely. I bless your trustworthy name, Lord, and I thank you for giving me the courage it takes to let go of the things I hold on to. It takes courage to trust you with them. So I pray for that courage—the courage to trust you. Help me let go, Lord. Give me the patience it takes to wait on your timing.

AMEN.

DAY 18:
When the Sun's Shining Down on Me

But let all who take refuge in you be glad; let them ever sing for joy. Spread your protection over them, that those who love your name may rejoice in you. For surely, O LORD, you bless the righteous; you surround them with your favor as with a shield.

—PSALM 5:11–12

God's name is a refuge.

Good or bad, rich or poor, male or female …
no matter who you are, the sun shines on you.

The sun knows no boundaries. The sun plays
no favorites. It just shines and shines, regardless of the moods of the people below. Even
when the weather blocks our view of the sun, it
still keeps on shining, patiently waiting for the
weather patterns to move out of its way.

Without the sun, our planet would be in big trouble.

God's name is the same way. For those of us
who love God's name, for those of us who are
righteous, God uses his name as a protective
covering over us. He is a refuge, spreading his
protection over us regardless of our moods, the
amount of money we have, or any other extenu-
ating circumstances.

Even when the storms of life threaten us and
block our view of God's protection, it is still
there, shining patiently down on us and keeping
us going in spite of its apparent disappearance.

Without God's protection, we would be in big trouble.

But his name is blessedly shining down upon us, sheltering us as with a shield. Blessed be that refuge.

Prayer for the Day:

O Lord, blessed be your name. I'm so thankful for your protection covering me, even when I don't see it. There are times in my life where I've forgotten about that protection, and I repent for that forgetfulness. Please help me to revel in your protection. I sing for joy and take refuge in you, Father God.

AMEN.

DAY 19:
When the World's All as It Should Be

I saw in heaven another great and marvelous sign: seven angels with the seven last plagues—last, because with them God's wrath is completed. And I saw what looked like a sea of glass mixed with fire and, standing beside the sea, those who had been victorious over the beast and his image and over the number of his name. They held harps given them by God and sang the song of Moses the servant of God and the song of the Lamb: "Great and marvelous are your deeds, Lord God Almighty. Just and true are your ways, King of the ages. Who will not fear you, O Lord, and bring glory to your name? For you alone are holy. All nations will come and worship before you, for your righteous acts have been revealed."

—REVELATION 15:1–4

God's name is eternal.

What a glimpse of the end of all days! Today's passage is an amazing word picture, recorded in the Bible to give us an idea of how this world will end and eternity will begin.

This is a good depiction of what the world should be like. This is a perfect world, where God has been victorious over his adversaries and all his righteous acts have been revealed.

And what is going on? People are praising God's name.

God's name is eternal, lasting beyond all our comprehension. His name will endure forever and ever and ever. There is no one who will not fear God and bring glory to his name at the end of time.

So, on this day, when we sing "Blessed Be Your Name," we are singing a song that we will continue to sing into eternity. God's name has outlasted us all. It began history and it will end history.

We are honored to sing of his name now, while we're given the choice.

Prayer for the Day:

O God Eternal, blessed is your name. I humbly bow before you and bless your name, your holy, everlasting name. I am hopeful in eternity, and I tremble at the thought of being able to speak your name in your presence. Nevertheless, I pray that you'll use me while I'm here on earth. Use me this day. Help me to make the most of my time, Lord.

AMEN.

DAY 20: Blessed Be Your Name

So Naaman went with his horses and chariots and stopped at the door of Elisha's house. Elisha sent a messenger to say to him, "Go, wash yourself seven times in the Jordan, and your flesh will be restored and you will be cleansed." But Naaman went away angry and said, "I thought that he would surely come out to me and stand and call on the name of the LORD his God, wave his hand over the spot and cure me of my leprosy. Are not Abana and Pharpar, the rivers of Damascus, better than any of the waters of Israel? Couldn't I wash in them and be cleansed?" So he turned and went off in a rage.

—2 KINGS 5:9–12

God's name is uncontrollable.

Naaman was a powerful soldier who had been afflicted with a very lowly disease: leprosy. But one of his servants told him about Elisha the prophet, a man who was known throughout the region for performing many mighty works through God's hand.

So Naaman contacted Elisha, who gave him a lowly remedy for his lowly affliction: bathing in the Jordan river. Naaman was incensed. Notice what he said: "I thought that [Elisha] would surely come out to me and stand and call on the name of the LORD his God, wave his hand over the spot and cure me of my leprosy."

Naaman thought he had it all figured out. He just knew that calling on God's name would be the answer. Easy. Right?

What Naaman didn't take into account was the attitude of his heart. God's name isn't some sort of magical talisman we can wave around for miracle cures. It is holy and sacred, and it doesn't always work the way we think it should.

God wanted Naaman to bathe in the Jordan river as a means of humbling his pride. Naaman couldn't see this right away and initially balked at the treatment Elisha prescribed for him. But, if we were to continue on with the passage, we'd learn that Naaman eventually went to the Jordan and was healed of his leprosy.

We can't always know how God will use his name, and we can't presuppose that we always have the answers.

God's name is uncontrollable, but it is always faithful. We don't know how God will respond to us, but we know that he will.

Prayer for the Day:

Almighty God, holy is your name. I praise and honor and bless your name, Lord. I pray that you'll encourage me in your name today, and that I would be able to see your will for my life today. Strengthen me so I may be fearless in following your direction, Lord, even if it contradicts my preconceived plans. Thank you, God.

AMEN.

DAY 21: Blessed Be Your Name

Ascribe to the LORD, O mighty ones, ascribe to the LORD glory and strength. Ascribe to the LORD the glory due his name; worship the LORD in the splendor of his holiness.

—PSALM 29:1-2

He who forms the mountains, creates the wind, and reveals his thoughts to man, he who turns dawn to darkness, and treads the high places of the earth—the LORD God Almighty is his name.

—AMOS 4:13

God's name is majestic.

Raise your hand if you've ever formed a mountain. Created a blustery north wind? How about turned the dawn into darkness, ever done that? Know anyone who has?

Of course not. These are things only God can do. His works are incomprehensible to our human minds. We can't even fathom the type of power it takes to form mountains, or create wind, or tread the high places of the earth. We've managed to create machines that can, in a sense, accomplish these things, but not on a grandiose, Almighty scale.

We have "earth-moving" machines, a pitiful name considering God's literal earth-moving power. Filmmakers and laboratory scientists use wind machines, but these only operate in closed environments and could never sweep across an entire country. Airplanes can take us to the high places of the earth, but again, they pale in comparison to God's power and only serve to remind us how small we really are.

And so we worship the Almighty God, because of his majesty and because of his awesome power.

Power that is summed up perfectly in his multi-faceted name.

Let us ascribe glory to God, glory and strength, because they are wholly due to him and him alone.

Prayer for the Day:

Almighty God, I'm bowled over in awe of your awesome power. Considering your greatness and all that you've done only serves to remind me how insignificant my own power is. But I also know that through you, I can do all things. I don't always understand your ways, Lord, but I'm thankful that I know you and that you are on my side. You are amazing.

AMEN.

DAY 22: On the Road Marked with Suffering

Remember how the enemy has mocked you, O Lord, how foolish people have reviled your name. Do not hand over the life of your dove to wild beasts; do not forget the lives of your afflicted people forever. Have regard for your covenant, because haunts of violence fill the dark places of the land. Do not let the oppressed retreat in disgrace; may the poor and needy praise your name.

—Psalm 74:18–21

I have told you these things, so that in me you may have peace. In this world you will have trouble. But take heart! I have overcome the world.

—John 16:33

God's name is an aid to the oppressed.

Jesus said it plainly in today's passage from John. We're going to have some troubled times. There's no getting around it. We live in a fallen world, and sometimes people are going to act evilly toward us. Sometimes we'll just find ourselves in a crummy situation that is no one's fault—it just stems from the fact that we aren't yet in a perfect world.

We'll have suffering in this world, there's no doubt about that. But we can call on the name of the Lord and he will readily aid us.

For some of us, suffering will take the form of snide remarks from unsaved coworkers. For others, it will take the form of financial hardships. For some, their suffering will result in death.

But Jesus commands us to take heart regardless of whatever our sufferings may be, because he has overcome the world. We needn't even fear death, because Jesus overcame even that part of this world.

Jesus won a victory for us, so we can call on his name in the midst of our suffering with the full knowledge that he will hear our cry and provide the exact help we need.

Prayer for the Day:

Dear God, I thank you for your rescuing name. I bless your name, Lord. I thank you that I can call on your name in the midst of my suffering; I thank you that your name is an aid to me when I'm oppressed. I know that you see me, Lord, and that when I call you, you answer in the way that you know is best. Thank you, Lord.

AMEN.

DAY 23:
On the
Road
Marked
with
Suffering

Dear friends, do not be surprised at the painful trial you are suffering, as though something strange were happening to you. But rejoice that you participate in the sufferings of Christ, so that you may be overjoyed when his glory is revealed. If you are insulted because of the name of Christ, you are blessed, for the Spirit of glory and of God rests on you. If you suffer, it should not be as a murderer or thief or any other kind of criminal, or even as a meddler. However, if you suffer as a Christian, do not be ashamed, but praise God that you bear that name.

—1 Peter 4:12–16

God's name is greater than our suffering.

Rejoice in suffering? Is Peter serious here? Could he actually mean that when we encounter suffering for being Christians, that we should literally rejoice about it?

Yes.

By being a standard-bearer for Christ, we will encounter suffering. But that suffering only serves to reveal his glory and is ultimately a blessing to us.

How, exactly? Because, according to Peter, when we suffer for the name of Christ, we'll find the Spirit of glory and of God resting upon us. Pretty comforting.

So, we needn't be ashamed of our suffering, but instead we need to praise God because we have the honor of bearing his name. The name itself is greater than our suffering will ever be.

His name is magnificent. It is a privilege to bear it and all that it contains. Jesus bore the name, and he suffered. Gloriously suffered.

We, too, bear the name, and we, too, will suffer. Maybe not to the same extent, but we know that when it comes, we somehow will have the ability to rejoice in it.

Prayer for the Day:

Dear Jesus, I'm so honored to bear your name. I bless that precious name. Jesus, I don't know if I'll encounter suffering today or not, but I'm thankful that when it does come, when I do suffer for your name's sake, that your Spirit rests upon me. I praise God that I bear your holy name. Your name is greater than my suffering.

AMEN.

DAY 24:
Though There's Pain in the Offering

When your people Israel have been defeated by an enemy because they have sinned against you and when they turn back and confess your name, praying and making supplication before you in this temple, then hear from heaven and forgive the sin of your people Israel and bring them back to the land you gave to them and their fathers.

—2 Chronicles 6:24–25

God's name is merciful.

When King Solomon had completed the temple he'd built for God, he prayed a prayer of dedication over it, which is what today's passage of Scripture comes from.

Being the insightful and wise king that he was, Solomon didn't say, "If, by some crazy, outside chance, the people just happen to sin against you—I know, it probably won't happen, but just in case it does …"

No. Solomon doesn't hedge his bets like that. He says, "When they sin …" Sinning is an eventuality. Solomon knew the Israelites wouldn't be able to live sin-free lives forever, and he knew they would lose some battles because of it.

So as he's dedicating the temple, he prays about just that eventuality and asks God to be merciful toward them when they show him contrition.

Talk about a painful offering.

Admitting sin is a painful thing, because of the consequences that often come with it. But this admission is a necessary offering that must be given to God in order to experience his forgiveness.

God is merciful, even in the midst of our most painful offerings.

Prayer for the Day:

Merciful God, I thank you and bless your name. God, I take this time to repent of my sin. I admit my wrongdoing, as painful as that may be. God, I turn back to you, I confess your name, and I make supplication before you right now. I thank you that you hear me and forgive me. I praise you for your mercy, Lord.

AMEN.

DAY 25: Blessed Be Your Name

*No one is like you, O L*ORD*; you are great, and your name is mighty in power. Who should not revere you, O King of* *the nations? This is your due. Among all the wise men of the nations and in all their kingdoms, there is no one like you.*

—JEREMIAH 10:6–7

God's name is unique.

What in this world is unique? One-of-a-kind? Those are words that are thrown around in marketing lingo and commercials so frequently that they have lost nearly all meaning, but is there really something completely unique in this world? Something that we could truthfully apply to the last sentence of today's passage?

Just God.

He is unique, as is his name. God is the only being in existence or nonexistence who is like himself. Nothing and no one else compares. The wisest man, the wealthiest king, the most powerful businessperson, the highest judge … these are all high positions, but they still pale when compared with God.

There is no one else like him. No one. None.

His name is mighty in power. He deserves our reverence. God's name deserves to be blessed and worshiped if only because there is no one else like him.

Prayer for the Day:

Dear Lord, you're beautiful. I bless your magnificent name. I see humanity desperately searching for the next unique, one-of-a-kind fad, and I realize that we're all actually searching for you. And there is no replacement for you; nothing that could ever exceed your majesty. You are mighty in power. I revere you, Lord. There is no one else like you.

AMEN.

DAY 26: You Give and Take Away

At this, Job got up and tore his robe and shaved his head. Then he fell to the ground in worship and said: "Naked I came from my mother's womb, and naked I will depart. The

Lord gave and the Lord has taken away; may the name of the Lord be praised."
In all this, Job did not sin by charging God with wrongdoing.

God's name is to be praised in all circumstances.

Job had just had the worst day of his life. All his livestock had been stolen or killed, his servants had been destroyed, and his children had all died when their house collapsed on them. And this all happened in one day.

Why?

Satan did it. Satan went to God, who gave him the ability to strike Job's wealth and family. God granted the authority in order to glorify his name, but Satan was the one who carried out the acts that resulted in Job's sorrow. Satan did it to try to get Job to deny God, but as we see from this passage, Satan's plan didn't work.

So was Job accurate in his statement that God gave and also took away his wealth and children? No, we know that was the Devil. But God understood where Job was coming from,

BLESSED BE YOUR NAME · 107

and he honored Job for it. God wasn't looking at the substance of Job's argument but rather the intent of his heart.

And God is the same way with us, when we praise his name regardless of whatever blessings or calamities we see in our lifetimes.

Prayer for the Day:

Heavenly Father, I praise your name. I thank you that you are consistent, looking at the intent of my heart throughout all the diverse circumstances that befall me. Give me the awareness and strength to praise your name in any of those circumstances. Through all the storms of life and all the sunny days; help me to praise your name.

AMEN.

DAY 27: You Give and Take Away

For God so loved the world that he gave his one and only Son, that whoever believes in him shall not perish but have eternal life. For God did not send his Son into the world to condemn the world, but to save the world through him.

—JOHN 3:16–17

The next day John saw Jesus coming toward him and said, "Look, the Lamb of God, who takes away the sin of the world! This is the one I meant when I said, 'A man who comes after me has surpassed me because he was before me.' I myself did not know him, but the reason I came baptizing with water was that he might be revealed to Israel."

—John 1:29–31

God's name is a reflection of his character.

The lyrics we're focusing on today are interesting ones. "You give and take away." Is this true? Does God really give and take away?

Oh, yes, he does.

Taking a look at the gospel of John, we see that God gave us his only son, Jesus. Why? So that Jesus, through his death on the cross, might take away our sin.

God gives and God takes away.

God gives us new life. He takes away our old lives of sin.

God gives us an abundant life, taking away our spiritually impoverished lives.

God gives us the honor of approaching him by taking away the barrier that separated us.

God gives good things and takes away bad things.

No wonder our hearts choose to bless God's name.

Prayer for the Day:

God, your name is blessed! Thank you for giving me Jesus. Thank you for taking away my sin. Thank you so much for giving and taking away. God, I pray that you'll help me to maintain the proper perspective of your character and that you'll help me to see the wonderful things you've given me and the awful things you've taken away from me. Thank you so much for your generosity.

AMEN.

DAY 28: My Heart Will Choose to Say

After we had been there a number of days, a prophet named Agabus came down from Judea. Coming over to us, he took Paul's belt, tied his own hands and feet with it and said, "The Holy Spirit says, 'In this way the Jews of Jerusalem will bind

the owner of this belt and will hand him over to the Gentiles."' When we heard
this, we and the people there pleaded with Paul not to go up to Jerusalem. Then
Paul answered, "Why are you weeping and breaking my heart? I am ready not
only to be bound, but also to die in Jerusalem for the name of the Lord Jesus."

—**Acts 21:10–13**

God's name is a good reason to live and to die.

Reading today's passage, there is no doubt about what Paul had chosen to say in his heart. His heart was ready for whatever would come his way.

Paul was staying with an evangelist in Caesarea, preparing to go into Jerusalem. He'd been compelled by the Spirit to go there, but the journey was long, and in every city he visited, the Holy Spirit warned him that he would face hardships and prison there. During his visit to the city of Tyre a few days previous, some disciples there urged Paul not to go to Jerusalem.

But Paul had his priorities in order. Even though he knew his upcoming trip would be dangerous, he was ready to go. In his heart, he'd chosen to bless the name of the Lord regardless of his own situation; he just wanted to preach that name.

And God honored him for it. He went to Jerusalem and soon found himself arrested and on trial for preaching the name of Jesus. But God blessed Paul's ministry even from prison and gave him an audience to preach the name of Jesus before the king of the region, Agrippa.

Paul had chosen in his heart to bless the name of God. God blessed him for it.

Prayer for the Day:

God, I bless your name. From the depths of my heart, I choose to bless your wonderful name. I don't know where this road of my life will lead me, but I'm thankful that you're accompanying me and ordering my steps. I pray that you will empower me with the ability and desire to continue to choose your name again and again, regardless of the hardships I might face. Help me to be a modern-day Paul, Lord.

AMEN.

DAY 29: Lord, Blessed Be Your Name

At the time of sacrifice, the prophet Elijah stepped forward and prayed: "O LORD, God of Abraham, Isaac and Israel, let it be known today that you are God in Israel and that I am your servant and have done all these things at your command. Answer me, O LORD, answer me, so these people will know that you, O LORD, are God, and that you are turning their hearts back again." Then the fire of the LORD fell and burned up the sacrifice, the wood, the stones and the soil, and also licked up the water in the trench. When all the people saw this, they fell prostrate and cried, "The LORD—he is God! The LORD—he is God!"

—1 KINGS 18:36–39

God's name is greater than any other name on earth.

It was a showdown of biblical proportions: God versus Baal, winner take all.

Here's the way it worked. Elijah the prophet had challenged the prophets of the false god Baal to a contest of sorts, to prove once and for all who served the true God. The challenge was to present an offering to each god, calling on that god's name. Whichever god sent fire from heaven to consume the offering would be declared the true God.

The prophets of Baal went first, and their efforts were pathetic. They cut themselves and screamed their voices hoarse calling on Baal, but of course nothing happened to their altar. No fire, no smoke. Nothing.

Then Elijah upped the ante by having his altar doused with water. He had servants dig a trench around it and fill the trench with water. There was water everywhere. But when Elijah called on God's name, God sent fire that consumed the offering and all the water around it. And the Bible says that everyone who saw it knew that the Lord was God.

Elijah called on the name of the Lord. The prophets of Baal called on the name of their god. Nothing happened for them; everything happened for Elijah. God's name is the one true godly name.

His name is greater than any other name.

Prayer for the Day:

God, I bless your great name. Lord, sometimes I forget how powerful you really are. Sometimes I set my eyes on false gods and their false powers, momentarily forgetting how useless they really are. Please help me to keep my eyes on you. Please teach me to remember that your name is greater than any other name in this earth that I might be tempted to call upon. I trust your great name, Lord.

AMEN.

DAY 30:
Lord, Blessed Be Your Name

"Therefore say to the house of Israel, 'This is what the Sovereign LORD says: It is not for your sake, O house of Israel, that I am going to do these things, but for the sake of my holy name, which you have profaned among the nations where you have gone. I will show the holiness of my great name, which has been profaned among the nations, the name you have profaned among them.

Then the nations will know that I am the LORD, declares the Sovereign LORD, when I show myself holy through you before their eyes."

—**EZEKIEL 36:22–23**

God's name is alive in us.

Amazing. It's difficult to understand God's ways sometimes, isn't it?

Here are the Israelites. God's chosen people. The Israelites were so closely associated with God that their wrongdoing actually had the effect of profaning God's name. Their misconduct gave God a bad name.

But instead of chiding them for it and disowning them, God says through the prophet Ezekiel that he's going to reinstate their holiness and reinstate his name. Why? Because they're his chosen people, and he's so earnest about having a good name that he's going to raise them up to show the nations how holy his name is.

Unbelievable.

It's astounding that God can still show his holiness through us, even when we aren't the best examples of it. Even when we fail him, when we don't act completely Christlike to those around us, God's name can still be blessed.

God's name is alive in us, and he takes it seriously. Seriously enough to use us, despite our broken sinfulness. Despite our weaknesses. Despite our missteps.

Blessed be his name!

Prayer for the Day:

Lord God, you are so holy. Your name is worthy to be praised. God, thank you for using me, even when I'm not the best example of your love. I am blown away by your graciousness, and I'm astounded and humbled that your name is alive in me. God, show me how to treasure your name, and help me never to forget how important your name is to you, and how important it should be to me. I love you, Lord.

AMEN.